THE VICTORIA AND ALBERT MUSEUM
CHINESE
COLLECTION
ADDRESS BOOK

EBURY PRESS STATIONERY

First published in 1991 by Ebury Press Stationery
An imprint of the Random Century Group
Random Century House, 20 Vauxhall Bridge Road, London SW1V 2SA

Also available: The Victoria & Albert Chinese Collection Postcard Album; The Victoria & Albert Chinese Collection Postcards

Set in Weiss by FMT Graphics Limited, Southwark, London
Printed and bound in Hong Kong

Designed by Nigel Partridge

ISBN 0 7126 4533 0

Cover illustration:
Detail of woman's robe, embroidery on gauze-banded plain weave silk, late 17th-18th century, early Qing dynasty.
Title page illustration:
Dish, cloisonné enamel, 18th century.

INTRODUCTION

In China, the elegant life at court and among the cultured élite stimulated a demand for luxury goods – porcelain, lacquerware, silk robes and furniture – ancient crafts which flourished under successive dynasties. Examples of each, as contained within this book, provide vivid evidence of the accomplishments of China's civilization. Craftsmen had achieved technical perfection in the development of porcelain and in the creation of hard and lustrous glazes more than 800 years earlier than in Europe. Similarly lacquer, providing a protective and watertight covering for wood, was a major art form by the Warring States period (475-221 BC). Quite alien to the West, where the lacquer tree was unknown, the arrival of lacquers in Europe at the beginning of the 17th century exerted a powerful influence on furniture-making.

Silk was a treasured and expensive fabric. Year after year the caravans toiled to and fro along the Silk Road carrying their luxury cargoes from China to the market-places of Europe and India. Silk was not the only commodity traded but it was one of the most important, commanding particularly high prices in Imperial Rome where China was known as the 'land of silk'. Centuries later, long after silkworm eggs had been smuggled into Byzantium and the Chinese monopoly on silk production broken, European merchants were still drawn by the lure of Chinese silk to undertake voyages of discovery around the Cape of Good Hope to trade at the port of Canton.

Traditional pattern elements were reproduced in different combinations on all media. This book includes examples of silk robes with motifs either embroidered or incorporated during weaving; carved and inlaid lacquer; and porcelain painted in enamels. Rather than isolating each element as a symbolic device, taken together as a tradition they 'encode a series of personal and social targets common to many individuals in Imperial China – long life, official position, wealth, happiness and male progeny'. A child's clothes would include those flowers, fruit or creatures representing a wish for protection from evil spirits, while a piece of porcelain or enamelled ware decorated with peaches and bats would convey wishes of good luck, happiness and longevity. Certain items did incorporate specific iconographical schemes, such as the robes worn by Taoist initiates and the twelve-symbol robes of the reigning emperor and his immediate family.

European trading concerns, such as the Honourable East India Company, began importing substantial quantities of Chinese goods into Britain from the late 17th century. Later, alongside the bulk cargoes of tea, silk and porcelain, specialized categories of material arrived which had been produced by the Chinese purely for export, to meet foreign demand. These included religious vestments, embroidered shawls and wallpaper, as pictured in this book. In the 19th and 20th centuries importers such as Liberty & Company reintroduced to England a variety of Chinese luxury goods, for example Chinese robes which were worn as evening coats or dressing gowns. This trade has been more or less continuous ever since, a testament to the popularity of the treasures of China.

AMANDA WARD,
Far Eastern Collection

For information about joining the V&A Club and the Friends of the V&A contact Marketing Office on 071-938 8365

HOURS OF OPENING
Mondays-Saturdays 10.00-17.50
Sundays 14.30-17.50
Closed Christmas Eve, Christmas Day, Boxing Day, New Year's Day and May Day Bank Holiday.

Empress, *one of a set of paintings illustrating Chinese life, watercolour on pith paper, c1900.*

Name

Address

☎

Name

Address

☎

Name

Address

☎

Name

Address

☎

Name

Address

☎

Name

Address

☎

Name

Address

☎

Name

Address

☎

Name

Address

☎

Name

Address

☎

Name

Address

☎

Name

Address

☎

Name

Address

☎

Name

Address

☎

Name

Address

☎

Name

Address

☎

Name

Address

☎

Name

Address

☎

Name

Address

☎

Name

Address

☎

Name

Address

☎

Name

Address

☎

Dish, painted enamel on copper, mid-18th century.

Name

Address

☎

Name

Address

☎

Name

Address

☎

Name

Address

☎

Name

Address

☎

Name

Address

☎

Name

Address

☎

Name

Address

☎

Name

Address

☎

Name

Address

☎

Name

Address

☎

Name

Address

☎

Name

Address

☎

Name

Address

☎

Name

Address

☎

Name

Address

☎

Name

Address

☎

Name

Address

☎

Name

Address

☎

Name

Address

☎

Name

Address

☎

Name

Address

☎

Name

Address

☎

Name

Address

☎

Cupboard, one of a pair, painted and inlaid lacquer, c1650-1700.

Name

Address

_____ ☎

Name

Address

_____ ☎

Name

Address

_____ ☎

Name

Address

_____ ☎

Name

Address

_____ ☎

Name

Address

_____ ☎

Name

Address

_____ ☎

Name

Address

_____ ☎

Name

Address

_____ ☎

Name

Address

_____ ☎

Name

Address

_____ ☎

Name

Address

_____ ☎

Name

Address

_____ ☎

Name

Address

_____ ☎

Name

Address

_____ ☎

Name

Address

_____ ☎

Name _____

Address _____

_____ ☎ _____

Name _____

Address _____

_____ ☎ _____

Name _____

Address _____

_____ ☎ _____

Name _____

Address _____

_____ ☎ _____

Name _____

Address _____

_____ ☎ _____

Name _____

Address _____

_____ ☎ _____

Name _____

Address _____

_____ ☎ _____

Name _____

Address _____

_____ ☎ _____

Shawl, embroidery on satin weave silk, late 19th century.

Name

Address

☎

Name

Address

☎

Name

Address

☎

Name

Address

☎

Name

Address

☎

Name

Address

☎

Name

Address

☎

Name

Address

☎

Name

Address

☎

Name

Address

☎

Name

Address

☎

Name

Address

☎

Name

Address

☎

Name

Address

☎

Name

Address

☎

Name

Address

☎

Name

Address

☎

Name

Address

☎

Name

Address

☎

Name

Address

☎

Name

Address

☎

Name

Address

☎

Name

Address

☎

Name

Address

☎

Dish, porcelain painted with basket of flowers and carp, c1740-1750.

Name

Address

☎

Name

Address

☎

Name

Address

☎

Name

Address

☎

Name

Address

☎

Name

Address

☎

Name

Address

☎

Name

Address

☎

Name

Address

☎

Name

Address

☎

Name

Address

☎

Name

Address

☎

Name

Address

☎

Name

Address

☎

Name

Address

☎

Name

Address

☎

Name

Address

☎

Name

Address

☎

Name

Address

☎

Name

Address

☎

Name

Address

☎

Name

Address

☎

Name

Address

☎

Name

Address

☎

Interior scene, from an album of paintings, watercolour on paper, c1820–1840.

Name

Address

☎

Name

Address

☎

Name

Address

☎

Name

Address

☎

Name

Address

☎

Name

Address

☎

Name

Address

☎

Name

Address

☎

Name _____

Address _____

_____ ☎ _____

Name _____

Address _____

_____ ☎ _____

Name _____

Address _____

_____ ☎ _____

Name _____

Address _____

_____ ☎ _____

Name _____

Address _____

_____ ☎ _____

Name _____

Address _____

_____ ☎ _____

Name _____

Address _____

_____ ☎ _____

Name

Address

☎

Name

Address

☎

Name

Address

☎

Name

Address

☎

Name

Address

☎

Name

Address

☎

Name

Address

☎

Name

Address

☎

Detail of panel of wallpaper, c1810–1830.

Name

Address

☎

Name

Address

☎

Name

Address

☎

Name

Address

☎

Name

Address

☎

Name

Address

☎

Name

Address

☎

Name

Address

☎

Name

Address

☎

Name

Address

☎

Name

Address

☎

Name

Address

☎

Name

Address

☎

Name

Address

☎

Name

Address

☎

Name

Address

☎

Name

Address

☎

Name

Address

☎

Name

Address

☎

Name

Address

☎

Name

Address

☎

Name

Address

☎

Name

Address

☎

Name

Address

☎

Vase and cover, cloisonné enamel on copper, Qianlong period, 1736–1795.

Name _____

Address _____

_____ ☎ _____

Name _____

Address _____

_____ ☎ _____

Name _____

Address _____

_____ ☎ _____

Name _____

Address _____

_____ ☎ _____

Name _____

Address _____

_____ ☎ _____

Name _____

Address _____

_____ ☎ _____

Name _____

Address _____

_____ ☎ _____

Name _____

Address _____

_____ ☎ _____

Name _____

Address _____

_____ ☎ _____

Name _____

Address _____

_____ ☎ _____

Name _____

Address _____

_____ ☎ _____

Name _____

Address _____

_____ ☎ _____

Name _____

Address _____

_____ ☎ _____

Name _____

Address _____

_____ ☎ _____

Name _____

Address _____

_____ ☎ _____

Name _____

Address _____

_____ ☎ _____

Name _____

Address _____

_____ ☎ _____

Name _____

Address _____

_____ ☎ _____

Name _____

Address _____

_____ ☎ _____

Name _____

Address _____

_____ ☎ _____

Name _____

Address _____

_____ ☎ _____

Name _____

Address _____

_____ ☎ _____

Name _____

Address _____

_____ ☎ _____

Name _____

Address _____

_____ ☎ _____

Shawl, silk crêpe decorated with silk embroidery, c1870-1920.

Name _____

Address _____

_____ ☎ _____

Name _____

Address _____

_____ ☎ _____

Name _____

Address _____

_____ ☎ _____

Name _____

Address _____

_____ ☎ _____

Name _____

Address _____

_____ ☎ _____

Name _____

Address _____

_____ ☎ _____

Name _____

Address _____

_____ ☎ _____

Name _____

Address _____

_____ ☎ _____

Name

Address

☎

Name

Address

☎

Name

Address

☎

Name

Address

☎

Name

Address

☎

Name

Address

☎

Name

Address

☎

Name

Address

☎

Name

Address

☎

Name

Address

☎

Name

Address

☎

Name

Address

☎

Name

Address

☎

Name

Address

☎

Name

Address

☎

Name

Address

☎

Lantern, porcelain decorated in enamels, 1725–1750.

Name _____

Address _____

_____ ☎ _____

Name _____

Address _____

_____ ☎ _____

Name _____

Address _____

_____ ☎ _____

Name _____

Address _____

_____ ☎ _____

Name _____

Address _____

_____ ☎ _____

Name _____

Address _____

_____ ☎ _____

Name _____

Address _____

_____ ☎ _____

Name _____

Address _____

_____ ☎ _____

Name _____

Address _____

_____ ☎ _____

Name _____

Address _____

_____ ☎ _____

Name _____

Address _____

_____ ☎ _____

Name _____

Address _____

_____ ☎ _____

Name _____

Address _____

_____ ☎ _____

Name _____

Address _____

_____ ☎ _____

Name _____

Address _____

_____ ☎ _____

Name _____

Address _____

_____ ☎ _____

Name

Address

☎

Name

Address

☎

Name

Address

☎

Name

Address

☎

Name

Address

☎

Name

Address

☎

Name

Address

☎

Name

Address

☎

Panel of painted silk, late 18th century.

Name

Address

☎

Name

Address

☎

Name

Address

☎

Name

Address

☎

Name

Address

☎

Name

Address

☎

Name

Address

☎

Name

Address

☎

Name _____

Address _____

_____ ☎ _____

Name _____

Address _____

_____ ☎ _____

Name _____

Address _____

_____ ☎ _____

Name _____

Address _____

_____ ☎ _____

Name _____

Address _____

_____ ☎ _____

Name _____

Address _____

_____ ☎ _____

Name _____

Address _____

_____ ☎ _____

Name _____

Address _____

_____ ☎ _____

Name _____

Address _____

_____ ☎ _____

Name _____

Address _____

_____ ☎ _____

Name _____

Address _____

_____ ☎ _____

Name _____

Address _____

_____ ☎ _____

Name _____

Address _____

_____ ☎ _____

Name _____

Address _____

_____ ☎ _____

Name _____

Address _____

_____ ☎ _____

Name _____

Address _____

_____ ☎ _____

Large dish, porcelain painted with flowers of the four seasons, Kangxi period, c1710-1722.

Name

Address

_____ ☎ _____

Name

Address

_____ ☎ _____

Name

Address

_____ ☎ _____

Name

Address

_____ ☎ _____

Name

Address

_____ ☎ _____

Name

Address

_____ ☎ _____

Name

Address

_____ ☎ _____

Name

Address

_____ ☎ _____

Name

Address

☎

Name

Address

☎

Name

Address

☎

Name

Address

☎

Name

Address

☎

Name

Address

☎

Name

Address

☎

Name

Address

☎

Name

Address

☎

Name

Address

☎

Name

Address

☎

Name

Address

☎

Name

Address

☎

Name

Address

☎

Name

Address

☎

Name

Address

☎

Military Archery Practice, *one of a series of drawings of court ceremonies and domestic scenes, watercolour on silk, c1850.*

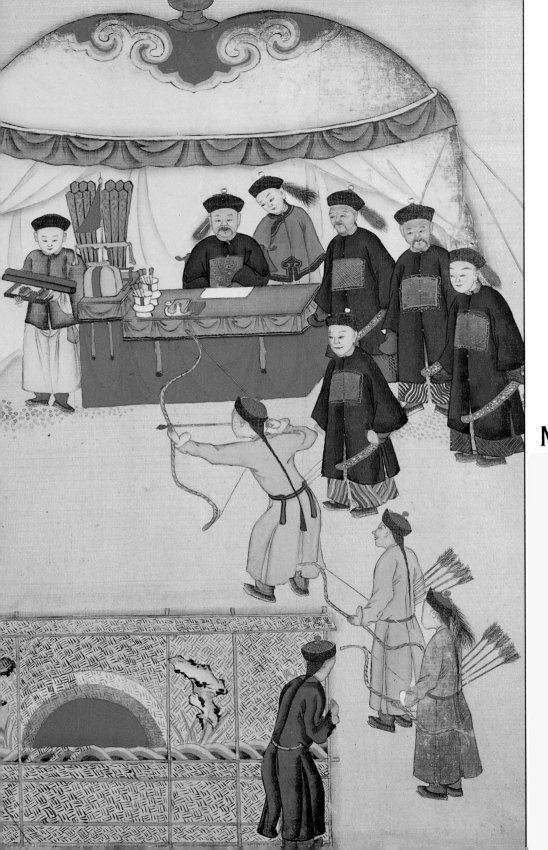

M

Name _____

Address _____

_____ ☎ _____

Name _____

Address _____

_____ ☎ _____

Name _____

Address _____

_____ ☎ _____

Name _____

Address _____

_____ ☎ _____

Name _____

Address _____

_____ ☎ _____

Name _____

Address _____

_____ ☎ _____

Name _____

Address _____

_____ ☎ _____

Name _____

Address _____

_____ ☎ _____

Name

Address

☎

Name

Address

☎

Name

Address

☎

Name

Address

☎

Name

Address

☎

Name

Address

☎

Name

Address

☎

Name

Address

☎

Name _____

Address _____

_____ ☎ _____

Name _____

Address _____

_____ ☎ _____

Name _____

Address _____

_____ ☎ _____

Name _____

Address _____

_____ ☎ _____

Name _____

Address _____

_____ ☎ _____

Name _____

Address _____

_____ ☎ _____

Name _____

Address _____

_____ ☎ _____

Name _____

Address _____

_____ ☎ _____

Pouch, embroidery on cream satin weave silk, late 19th to early 20th century.

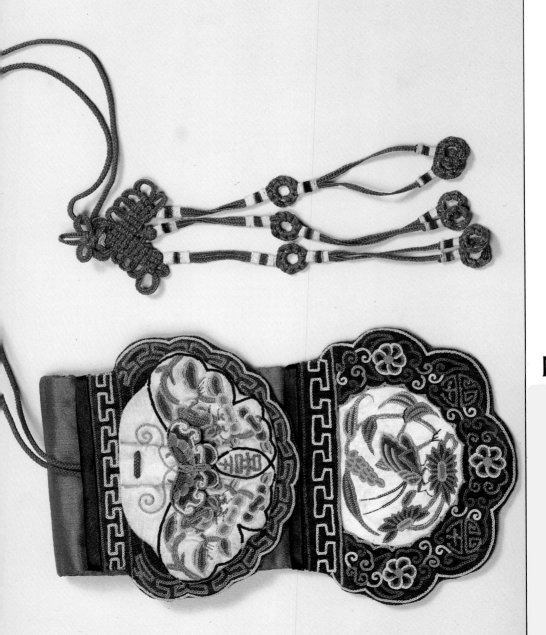

Name

Address

☎

Name

Address

☎

Name

Address

☎

Name

Address

☎

Name

Address

☎

Name

Address

☎

Name

Address

☎

Name

Address

☎

Name _____

Address _____

_____ ☎ _____

Name _____

Address _____

_____ ☎ _____

Name _____

Address _____

_____ ☎ _____

Name _____

Address _____

_____ ☎ _____

Name _____

Address _____

_____ ☎ _____

Name _____

Address _____

_____ ☎ _____

Name _____

Address _____

_____ ☎ _____

Name _____

Address _____

_____ ☎ _____

Name

Address

☎

Name

Address

☎

Name

Address

☎

Name

Address

☎

Name

Address

☎

Name

Address

☎

Name

Address

☎

Name

Address

☎

Back view of Taoist robe, embroidery on satin weave silk, Qing dynasty, 18th century.

O

Name

Address

☎

Name

Address

☎

Name

Address

☎

Name

Address

☎

Name

Address

☎

Name

Address

☎

Name

Address

☎

Name

Address

☎

Name

Address

☎

Name

Address

☎

Name

Address

☎

Name

Address

☎

Name

Address

☎

Name

Address

☎

Name

Address

☎

Name

Address

☎

Name _____

Address _____

_____ ☎ _____

Name _____

Address _____

_____ ☎ _____

Name _____

Address _____

_____ ☎ _____

Name _____

Address _____

_____ ☎ _____

Name _____

Address _____

_____ ☎ _____

Name _____

Address _____

_____ ☎ _____

Name _____

Address _____

_____ ☎ _____

Name _____

Address _____

_____ ☎ _____

Woman's overgarment, embroidery on satin weave silk, late 18th to early 19th century.

P

Name

Address

☎

Name

Address

☎

Name

Address

☎

Name

Address

☎

Name

Address

☎

Name

Address

☎

Name

Address

☎

Name

Address

☎

Name

Address

☎

Name

Address

☎

Name

Address

☎

Name

Address

☎

Name

Address

☎

Name

Address

☎

Name

Address

☎

Name

Address

☎

Name

Address

☎

Name

Address

☎

Name

Address

☎

Name

Address

☎

Name

Address

☎

Name

Address

☎

Name

Address

☎

Name

Address

☎

Detail of a Manchu woman's robe, embroidery on twill weave silk, 19th century.

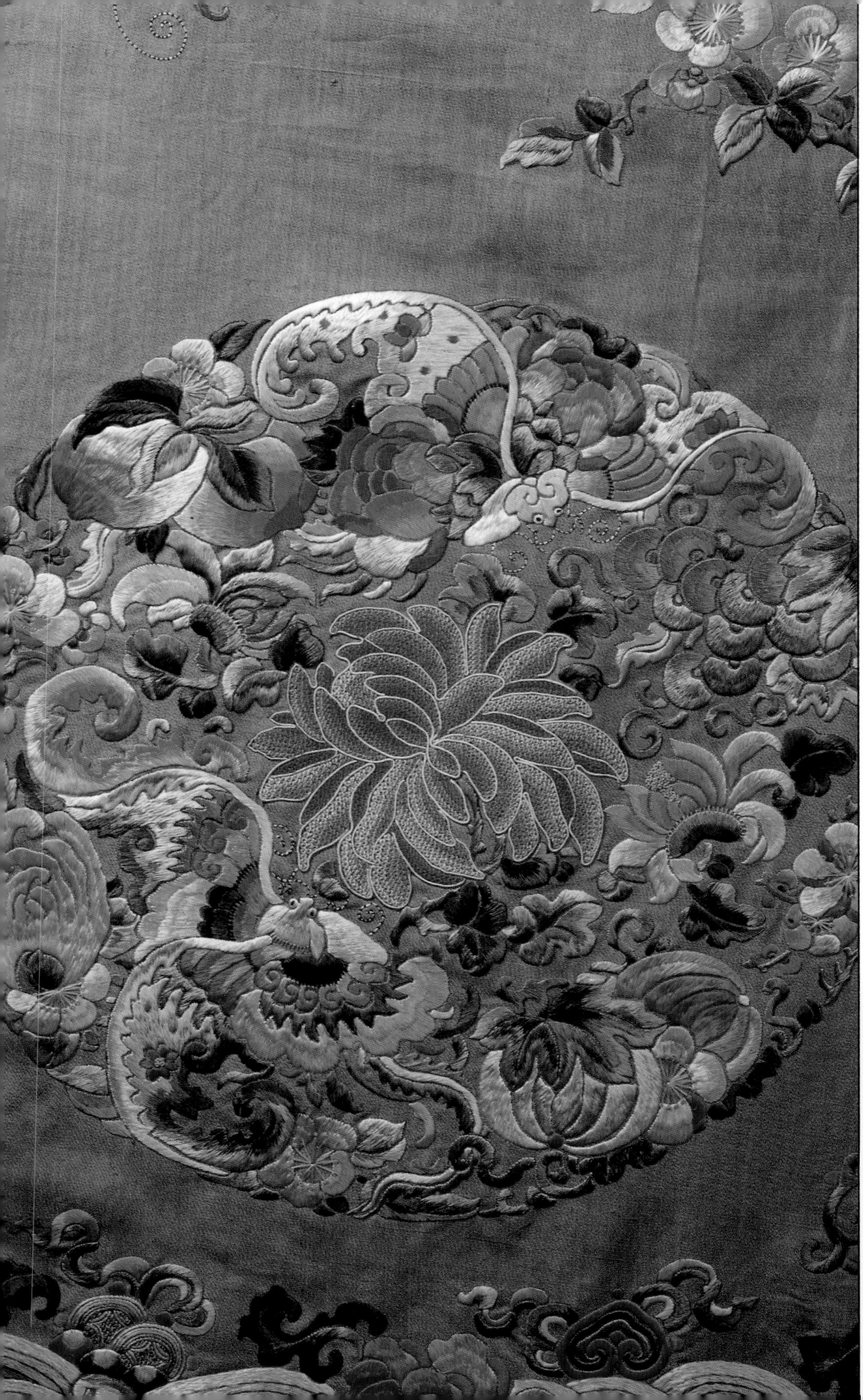

Q

Name

Address

☎

Name

Address

☎

Name

Address

☎

Name

Address

☎

Name

Address

☎

Name

Address

☎

Name

Address

☎

Name

Address

☎

Name

Address

☎

Name

Address

☎

Name

Address

☎

Name

Address

☎

Name

Address

☎

Name

Address

☎

Name

Address

☎

Name

Address

☎

Name

Address

☎

Name

Address

☎

Name

Address

☎

Name

Address

☎

Name

Address

☎

Name

Address

☎

Name

Address

☎

Name

Address

☎

Interior scene, from an album of paintings, watercolour on paper, c1820–1840.

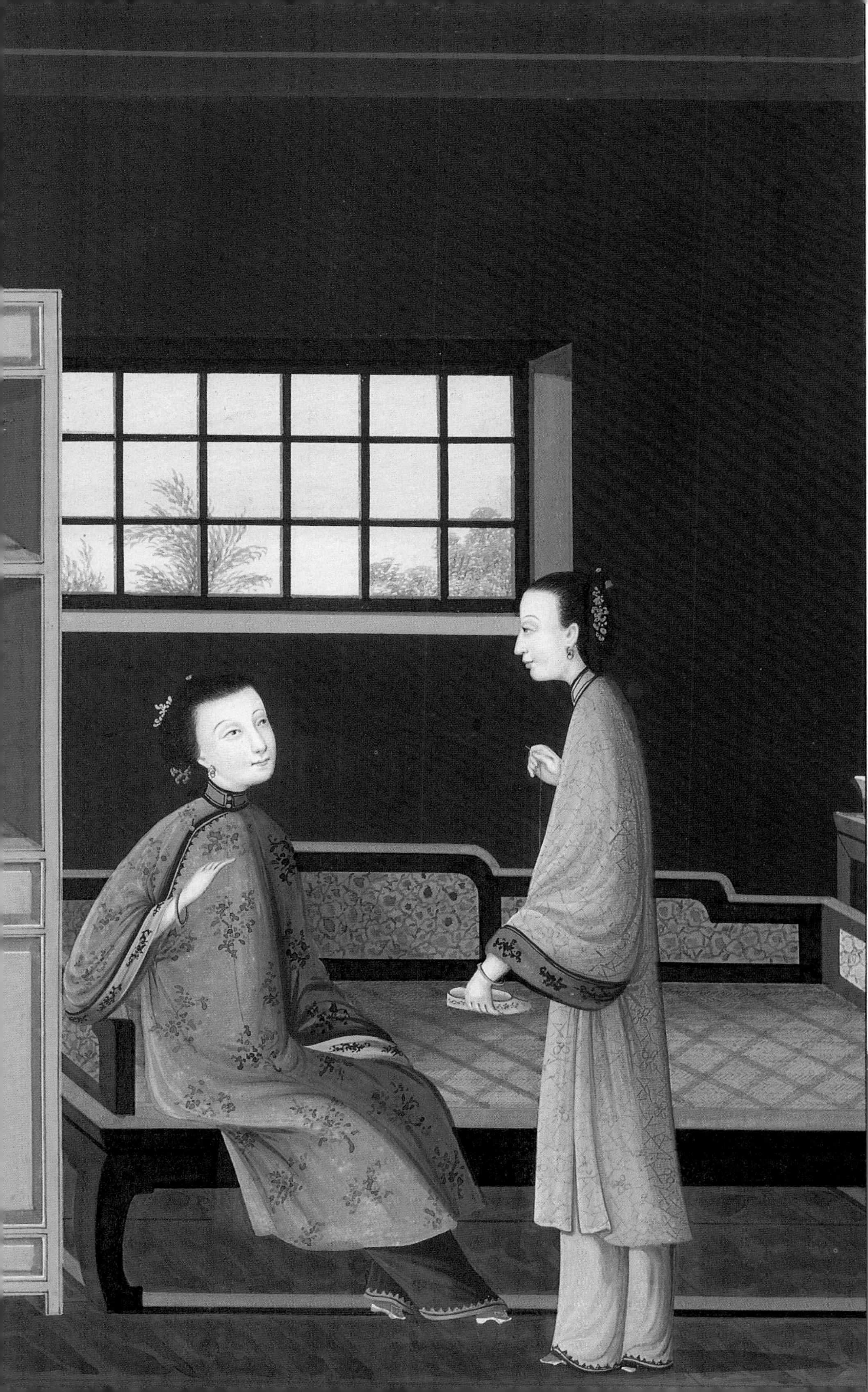

R

Name

Address

_____ ☎ _____

Name

Address

_____ ☎ _____

Name

Address

_____ ☎ _____

Name

Address

_____ ☎ _____

Name

Address

_____ ☎ _____

Name

Address

_____ ☎ _____

Name

Address

_____ ☎ _____

Name

Address

_____ ☎ _____

Name

Address

☎

Name

Address

☎

Name

Address

☎

Name

Address

☎

Name

Address

☎

Name

Address

☎

Name

Address

☎

Name

Address

☎

Name _____

Address _____

_____ ☎ _____

Name _____

Address _____

_____ ☎ _____

Name _____

Address _____

_____ ☎ _____

Name _____

Address _____

_____ ☎ _____

Name _____

Address _____

_____ ☎ _____

Name _____

Address _____

_____ ☎ _____

Name _____

Address _____

_____ ☎ _____

Name _____

Address _____

_____ ☎ _____

Dish, porcelain painted with birds, butterflies and flowers, c1820-1850.

S

Name

Address

☎

Name

Address

☎

Name

Address

☎

Name

Address

☎

Name

Address

☎

Name

Address

☎

Name

Address

☎

Name

Address

☎

Name

Address

☎

Name

Address

☎

Name

Address

☎

Name

Address

☎

Name

Address

☎

Name

Address

☎

Name

Address

☎

Name

Address

☎

Name _____

Address _____

_____ ☎ _____

Name _____

Address _____

_____ ☎ _____

Name _____

Address _____

_____ ☎ _____

Name _____

Address _____

_____ ☎ _____

Name _____

Address _____

_____ ☎ _____

Name _____

Address _____

_____ ☎ _____

Name _____

Address _____

_____ ☎ _____

Name _____

Address _____

_____ ☎ _____

Pair of Rank Badges, embroidery on satin weave silk, late 18th to early 19th century.

T

Name

Address

☏

Name

Address

☏

Name

Address

☏

Name

Address

☏

Name

Address

☏

Name

Address

☏

Name

Address

☏

Name

Address

☏

Name

Address

☎

Name

Address

☎

Name

Address

☎

Name

Address

☎

Name

Address

☎

Name

Address

☎

Name

Address

☎

Name

Address

☎

Name _____

Address _____

_____ ☎ _____

Name _____

Address _____

_____ ☎ _____

Name _____

Address _____

_____ ☎ _____

Name _____

Address _____

_____ ☎ _____

Name _____

Address _____

_____ ☎ _____

Name _____

Address _____

_____ ☎ _____

Name _____

Address _____

_____ ☎ _____

Name _____

Address _____

_____ ☎ _____

Large vase, porcelain decorated in enamels, c1770-1795.

Name

Address

☎

Name

Address

☎

Name

Address

☎

Name

Address

☎

Name

Address

☎

Name

Address

☎

Name

Address

☎

Name

Address

☎

Name

Address

☎

Name

Address

☎

Name

Address

☎

Name

Address

☎

Name

Address

☎

Name

Address

☎

Name

Address

☎

Name

Address

☎

Name _____

Address _____

_____ ☎ _____

Name _____

Address _____

_____ ☎ _____

Name _____

Address _____

_____ ☎ _____

Name _____

Address _____

_____ ☎ _____

Name _____

Address _____

_____ ☎ _____

Name _____

Address _____

_____ ☎ _____

Name _____

Address _____

_____ ☎ _____

Name _____

Address _____

_____ ☎ _____

Hanging, painted silk gauze, c1820-1840.

V

Name

Address

☎

Name

Address

☎

Name

Address

☎

Name

Address

☎

Name

Address

☎

Name

Address

☎

Name

Address

☎

Name

Address

☎

Name _____

Address _____

_____ ☎ _____

Name _____

Address _____

_____ ☎ _____

Name _____

Address _____

_____ ☎ _____

Name _____

Address _____

_____ ☎ _____

Name _____

Address _____

_____ ☎ _____

Name _____

Address _____

_____ ☎ _____

Name _____

Address _____

_____ ☎ _____

Name _____

Address _____

_____ ☎ _____

Name

Address

☎

Name

Address

☎

Name

Address

☎

Name

Address

☎

Name

Address

☎

Name

Address

☎

Name

Address

☎

Name

Address

☎

Painted red lacquer box, Ming dynasty, dated 1600 AD.

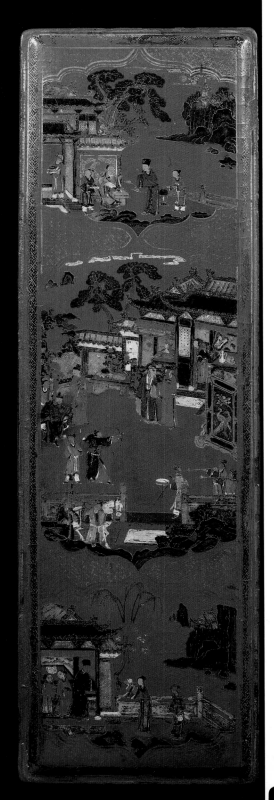

Name

Address

☎

Name

Address

☎

Name

Address

☎

Name

Address

☎

Name

Address

☎

Name

Address

☎

Name

Address

☎

Name

Address

☎

Name

Address

☎

Name

Address

☎

Name

Address

☎

Name

Address

☎

Name

Address

☎

Name

Address

☎

Name

Address

☎

Name

Address

☎

Name _____

Address _____

_____ ☎ _____

Name _____

Address _____

_____ ☎ _____

Name _____

Address _____

_____ ☎ _____

Name _____

Address _____

_____ ☎ _____

Name _____

Address _____

_____ ☎ _____

Name _____

Address _____

_____ ☎ _____

Name _____

Address _____

_____ ☎ _____

Name _____

Address _____

_____ ☎ _____

Detail of twelve-symbol robe, embroidery on satin weave silk, 19th century.

YZ

Name

Address

☎

Name

Address

☎

Name

Address

☎

Name

Address

☎

Name

Address

☎

Name

Address

☎

Name

Address

☎

Name

Address

☎

Name _____

Address _____

_____ ☎ _____

Name _____

Address _____

_____ ☎ _____

Name _____

Address _____

_____ ☎ _____

Name _____

Address _____

_____ ☎ _____

Name _____

Address _____

_____ ☎ _____

Name _____

Address _____

_____ ☎ _____

Name _____

Address _____

_____ ☎ _____

Name _____

Address _____

_____ ☎ _____

Name

Address

☎

Name

Address

☎

Name

Address

☎

Name

Address

☎

Name

Address

☎

Name

Address

☎

Name

Address

☎